CONTENTS

Introduction

1: The Birth of a Legend (1941)

2: Triumph and Expansion During World War II

3: Post-War Revival and the Malayan Emergency

4: Mastering Counter-Insurgency and Global Operations

5: Northern Ireland and the Troubles (1969-1998)

6: The Iranian Embassy Siege (1980)

7: The Falklands War (1982)

8: The Gulf War and Desert Operations

9: Post 9/11 Operations

10: Training, Selection and the Making of an SAS Soldier

11: The SAS in Popular Culture

12: Legacy and Influence

Conclusion

Introduction

The SAS: A Legacy of Bravery and Innovation

It was a moonless night in November 1941 when a handful of British soldiers, clad in desert khaki and armed with little more than determination and daring, prepared to jump into the unknown. Above the Libyan desert, their aircraft bucked against the wind, the roar of its engines a defiant heartbeat in the vast emptiness of the night. They were volunteers for a new, untried force—a creation born not from the cautious minds of military strategists, but from the audacious vision of one man: David Stirling.

As they leapt into the dark, they carried with them an idea as dangerous as the explosives strapped to their backs: that small, mobile teams of men could wreak havoc deep behind enemy lines, striking with speed and precision where the enemy felt safest. It was an idea that would forever change the nature of warfare.

From its perilous beginnings in the deserts of North Africa to its legendary triumphs in Europe, Asia, and beyond, the Special Air Service (SAS) has become synonymous with ingenuity, endurance, and the indomitable spirit of human courage. Its story is a testament to the power of adaptability—of turning adversity into opportunity and innovation into victory.

Who Dares Wins: The Motto that Defines Elite Warfare

The motto *Who Dares Wins* was not chosen lightly. It encapsulates a philosophy that has been at the heart of the SAS since its inception—a belief that boldness, when married to skill and preparation, can achieve the impossible. This creed has guided the SAS through some of history's most daring missions: sabotaging enemy planes under the scorching sun of North Africa, storming the Iranian Embassy under the gaze of the world's cameras, and hunting Scud missiles in the perilous expanse of the Iraqi desert.

But daring alone is not enough. Behind every dramatic success lies meticulous planning, ruthless training, and a relentless pursuit of excellence. The men of the SAS are not born exceptional; they are forged through a brutal selection process that breaks all but the most determined. They are thinkers and warriors, strategists and soldiers—masters of a craft that blends intellect with physical prowess.

This book is the story of that craft. It is a journey through the pivotal moments that shaped the SAS, exploring how it evolved from a desperate gamble in the sands of North Africa into the blueprint for modern special forces around the world. It is a tale of audacity, ingenuity, and sacrifice—of the men who dared, and the victories they won.

Prepare to enter a world where the line between success and failure is razor-thin, where the difference between life and death often hinges on a single decision. This is the story of the SAS.

Chapter 1: The Birth of a Legend (1941)

David Stirling's Vision

It began, as so many stories of extraordinary human endeavor do, with failure. In early 1941, Lieutenant David Stirling found himself lying in a hospital bed in Cairo, his body battered, his future uncertain. He was recovering from a parachuting accident—a moment of hubris that had gone spectacularly wrong. What had been intended as a bold leap of faith became an ignominious collapse into the Egyptian sand, leaving Stirling with a back injury and time to think.

For most men, such a setback would have marked the end of ambition. For Stirling, it was only the beginning. He was not an obvious candidate for military greatness. Tall, languid, and prone to rebellion, he had stumbled his way into the British Army with little sense of direction. Yet behind the aristocratic nonchalance lay a mind that thrived on unconventional thinking. Stirling's injury became his crucible, forging a radical idea that would challenge the very foundations of British military doctrine.

The conventional wisdom of the day was clear: victory required overwhelming force. Armies moved in vast columns; battles were fought on clearly defined frontlines. But in the sprawling, sun-scorched wilderness of North Africa, this approach had proven disastrous. The German Afrika Korps, led by the brilliant and elusive General Erwin Rommel, outmanoeuvred their enemies with devastating efficiency. Stirling believed there was another way—one that eschewed brute force for stealth and audacity.

His vision was simple in its daring. A small, highly trained force could slip behind enemy lines, striking at vital targets—airfields, supply depots, and communication centers—with speed and precision. The aim was not to hold ground but to sow chaos, forcing the enemy to divert resources and live in perpetual fear of attack. It was a strategy that defied tradition, and its champion was an unorthodox figure in every sense.

The North African Campaign

The North African desert was a landscape of extremes—searing heat by day, bitter cold by night, and vast horizons that could swallow a man whole. It was a place where survival depended on ingenuity and endurance, qualities Stirling's new force would soon be called upon to demonstrate in abundance.

Their first mission, a parachute drop behind German lines in November 1941, was a baptism of fire. Everything that could go wrong did. High winds scattered the men across the desert, turning a coordinated assault into a desperate struggle for survival. Equipment was lost, and several soldiers were captured or killed. Stirling's grand vision seemed destined for ruin before it had even begun.

But failure breeds adaptation. Recognising the limitations of parachute deployment, Stirling forged an alliance with the Long Range Desert Group (LRDG), a reconnaissance unit skilled in navigating the treacherous terrain. Together, they devised a new approach—using specially modified jeeps to penetrate enemy territory. These lightweight vehicles, bristling with machine guns, became the chariots of a new kind of warfare.

Early Challenges and First Raids

The raid on Tamet airfield was the moment the legend began to take shape. Under the cover of night, Stirling's men crept into the German-held base, planting explosives on aircraft and fuel stores. By dawn, more than thirty planes had been destroyed, a crippling blow to the Luftwaffe's air superiority. The mission was a triumph of ingenuity and daring, executed with a precision that left the enemy reeling.

Yet the true genius of the operation lay not in its execution but in its implications. Stirling had demonstrated that a handful of men, operating independently of the lumbering machinery of conventional war, could achieve results out of all proportion to their numbers. It was warfare as guerrilla art—fluid, unpredictable, and devastating.

Recruiting for the new unit was unlike anything the British Army had ever seen. Stirling sought men who could think as well as fight—individuals with the courage to defy orders when necessary and the resourcefulness to survive in the harshest conditions. Many were misfits, men who chafed against military discipline but thrived in the chaos of battle. Their training was brutal, designed to weed out the faint of heart and forge a brotherhood of warriors whose loyalty was to each other, not to rank or protocol.

The desert became their crucible, and Stirling their philosopher-commander, weaving a vision of war that was part poetry, part pragmatism. Every raid was a dance of danger and deception, a calculated gamble where the stakes were always life and death.

A New Era of Warfare

As 1942 dawned, the tide of war in North Africa began to shift. The SAS—still a fledgling force, barely acknowledged by the wider military establishment—had proven its worth. Its operations disrupted supply lines, destroyed vital infrastructure, and eroded the enemy's sense of security. Stirling's vision had become a reality, and the Special Air Service was on the brink of legend.

But this was only the beginning.

Chapter 2: Triumph and Expansion During World War II

Paddy Mayne's Command

If David Stirling was the philosophical architect of the SAS, then Robert "Paddy" Mayne was its ferocious spirit. Where Stirling was calm and calculating, Mayne burned with volcanic intensity —a man of towering physicality and legendary ferocity. A former Irish rugby international, Mayne's capacity for violence was matched only by his brilliance in battle. His exploits would become the stuff of myth, but behind every dramatic tale lay a razor-sharp mind and an unbreakable will.

When Stirling was captured by German forces in January 1943, the future of the SAS hung by a thread. Without its founder, the unit could have disintegrated into chaos or been absorbed back into the conventional military. Instead, under Mayne's leadership, it grew even deadlier. His aggressive tactics and disregard for bureaucratic interference made the SAS a force of relentless destruction. He turned raids into symphonies of devastation, striking with such fury that the enemy never knew what hit them.

Mayne's command was characterised by an unrelenting focus on the mission and a fierce loyalty to his men. He led from the front, often driving the jeep himself as he unleashed fire on enemy columns. His presence inspired both fear and awe—a leader who seemed almost mythical, a man who could drink all night, fight all day, and emerge victorious against impossible odds.

Raids Across Europe and the Mediterranean

With North Africa secured, the SAS was unleashed on a broader canvas. Europe and the Mediterranean became their new hunting grounds. From the olive groves of Italy to the hedgerows of France, their operations grew in scale and ambition. The destruction of vital supply lines, railway networks, and fuel depots became their stock-in-trade. They operated in small, mobile units—men who could disappear into the countryside as swiftly as they had struck.

The raid on the Italian airfield at Trapani in 1943 epitomised the SAS's ability to blend guile with ferocity. Disguised as Italian officers, a team led by Mayne infiltrated the base, placing charges on aircraft with such calm precision that they appeared to be conducting routine inspections. The resulting explosion was heard for miles, and the Luftwaffe's air power in the region was crippled.

The success of the SAS drew the admiration of Allied command and the fury of the enemy. In response, Adolf Hitler issued the infamous *Kommandobefehl*—an order to execute captured commandos without trial. It was a brutal decree, but one that only hardened the resolve of Stirling's and Mayne's men. For them, the war had become personal, a contest of wills where no quarter was asked, and none was given.

The SAS in France and Italy

As the Allies prepared for the liberation of France, the SAS was tasked with a crucial role in the clandestine war that would pave the way for D-Day. Dropped into the French countryside, their mission was to disrupt German reinforcements and assist the burgeoning resistance. It was warfare at its most perilous. Every village, every farmhouse could conceal a collaborator or an informer. Capture meant torture and death.

Yet it was in this unforgiving theatre that the SAS truly came into its own. The night raids on German supply convoys, the sabotage of key railway lines, and the ambushes that bled enemy divisions of men and materiel—all were executed with ruthless precision. The SAS became ghosts in the landscape, a force that seemed to materialise from the shadows only to vanish again, leaving destruction in their wake.

In Italy, the terrain was no less challenging. Mountain passes and narrow valleys turned every operation into a test of endurance and ingenuity. The SAS worked alongside partisans, striking at the heart of German occupation forces. Their raids were surgical, targeting bridges, fuel dumps, and command posts. In the harsh winter of 1944, their resilience was pushed to its limits, but their impact was undeniable.

The War's End: Disbandment and Recognition

As the guns of World War II fell silent in 1945, the SAS stood as one of the most decorated units in British military history. Yet, paradoxically, victory brought with it an existential threat. The very success of the SAS, born out of the unconventional needs of a world at war, made it seem obsolete in peacetime. In October 1945, the unit was officially disbanded, its future uncertain.

For the men who had fought in its ranks, the end was bittersweet. They had forged a brotherhood in the crucible of conflict, bound not by rank or uniform but by shared risk and shared triumph. Many returned to civilian life carrying the scars—seen and unseen—of battles fought in the shadows.

But legends are not so easily extinguished. Even as the SAS faded from the official order of battle, its spirit endured in the hearts of those who had served. The lessons they had learned—the value of agility, the power of surprise, the primacy of courage—would not be forgotten. The seeds of a future revival had already been sown.

Chapter 3: Post-War Revival and the Malayan Emergency

The Rebirth of the SAS (1947)

As the dust of the Second World War settled, the men who had been the bedrock of the SAS found themselves scattered across the globe, returning to civilian life or moving into other branches of the military. The unit's fame, though growing, was overshadowed by the larger scale of post-war reorganisation. But the SAS had a power more resilient than bureaucracy—its very nature had been forged in defiance of conventionality, and it could not be so easily dismantled.

The British Army's realisation that the tactics and brilliance of the SAS had been invaluable in the fight against a highly organised and resourceful enemy like Nazi Germany did not go unnoticed. Stirling, now a wounded hero, was determined to resurrect the unit, believing that the principles that had made the SAS so formidable in World War II could be adapted to a new kind of conflict—the kind that was already beginning to rear its ugly head across the globe.

It was in the jungles of Malaya that the SAS would find its rebirth. The Malayan Emergency (1948–1960) was an ideological battle as much as a military one—a brutal fight against communist insurgents that sought to turn the region into a Soviet ally. Britain, weary from war and struggling to maintain its empire, had to adapt. The military might that had crushed the Axis powers could not hope to defeat guerrilla forces hidden in the jungle, waiting to strike from the shadows. It required a different kind of warfare—smaller, stealthier, and infinitely more patient.

And so, with the re-establishment of the SAS in 1947, the principles of unconventional warfare would evolve further, setting the stage for its enduring legacy. Stirling and his men, familiar with the art of raiding behind enemy lines, would now fight an entirely new battle: counter-insurgency.

Counter-Insurgency Tactics in the Jungle

The jungles of Malaya were a world apart from the deserts of North Africa or the battlefields of Europe. The air was thick with moisture, the scent of earth and decay clinging to everything. Visibility was often reduced to mere feet, and every step could be the last. It was an unforgiving environment, perfect for an enemy who thrived on silence, stealth, and deception.

The Malayan communist insurgents, known as the Malayan Races Liberation Army (MRLA), had perfected the art of jungle warfare. They had the terrain on their side and were skilled in ambush tactics, slipping in and out of the foliage without a trace. They understood that the war was not about capturing territory, but about eroding the will of the British to maintain their presence.

The SAS, however, had its own advantages. Stirling's training program emphasised the importance of stealth, observation, and precision. Unlike conventional military units, which were trained to hold ground and engage in direct confrontation, the SAS worked in smaller groups, relying on surprise and their ability to disappear into the environment.

The SAS's role in Malaya was not to fight the enemy head-on, but to become part of the landscape. They did not chase after the communist forces; they tracked them, shadowed them, and waited. Ambushes, surprise attacks, and sabotage became their signature tactics. Every mission was a lesson in patience.

In 1950, a small SAS team, operating deep within the jungle, was tasked with locating and neutralising a key communist leader. The operation lasted for weeks, the men living off the land, moving under the cover of darkness. It was a war of attrition, and for every success there were casualties—men who had been swallowed by the jungle, their lives claimed by the very same forces they were fighting against.

Yet, even in such dire conditions, the SAS thrived. Their tactics were a textbook example of counter-insurgency at its finest. Rather than pushing forward and risking direct conflict, the SAS worked in concert with local forces, establishing intelligence networks and assisting in the formation of a Malay Anti-Communist Security Force. They never left a trail to follow, making it impossible for the enemy to predict their movements. And as the war dragged on, the communist forces began to lose ground.

Lessons from Malaya: Small Unit Tactics

The success of the SAS in Malaya was a triumph not just of superior tactics but also of strategy. In contrast to the larger, slower-moving units of the conventional military, the SAS excelled in small, highly mobile teams that could deploy quickly and decisively. This model, which had been perfected in the deserts of North Africa, proved to be just as effective in the jungles of Malaya.

One of the critical lessons the SAS learned from Malaya was the value of self-reliance. Each soldier was trained to perform multiple roles—whether it was tracking, combat, or intelligence gathering. The concept of the 'self-contained unit' became the cornerstone of SAS operations. In the jungle, there was no room for error. The smallest mistake could have catastrophic consequences. A team that was highly independent, yet able to function as a cohesive whole, was essential for survival.

The SAS also discovered that winning the hearts and minds of the local population was just as important as winning on the battlefield. In Malaya, the communist insurgents relied heavily on support from local villagers who were disillusioned with the

British presence. The SAS understood that defeating the insurgents wasn't enough; they had to cut off the insurgents' support network. They worked with local villagers, provided security, and in some cases, offered support for agriculture and basic needs.

By the time the Emergency officially ended in 1960, the SAS had proven its worth once again. The skills they honed in the jungles of Malaya would go on to define the unit's future operations in even more complex and perilous environments.

Chapter 4: Mastering Counter-Insurgency and Global Operations

Campaigns in Oman, Borneo, and Aden

In the years following the success in Malaya, the SAS found itself increasingly drawn into the far-flung conflicts that defined the mid-20th century. The world was in flux, as former colonies struggled for independence and Cold War tensions crept across the globe. Yet, in this chaotic environment, the SAS would be called upon to apply its unique skills in a variety of settings, each with its own challenges, but all offering opportunities to refine its craft of small-unit warfare.

The 1950s and 1960s saw the SAS deploy to the Middle East, Southeast Asia, and Africa, facing new enemies and new terrains. The lessons learned in Malaya would become the foundation for operations in Oman, Borneo, and Aden—each a microcosm of the global struggles for power, independence, and survival.

In Oman, the SAS found itself battling the communist insurgents of the Dhofar region, who were backed by the People's Democratic Republic of Yemen. The Sultan of Oman, a monarch whose rule was increasingly threatened by both internal and external forces, called upon British assistance. What followed was a conflict characterised by its isolation and the ruggedness of the terrain. The SAS, as always, was the ideal force for such an environment—highly mobile, deeply familiar with the art of jungle warfare, and experienced in working with local forces.

By the time they were called into action, the insurgents had already established strongholds within Oman's mountainous terrain, relying on the support of local tribes and external backing from the Soviet Union. The British army, with its more conventional methods, had struggled to contain the rebels. Yet, the SAS's ability to operate covertly in hostile environments made it the perfect force to tip the scales.

The SAS's role in Oman, particularly in the operation known as the "Jebel Akhdar" campaign, was to assist the Sultan's forces in clearing rebel positions deep within the mountains. It was a war of attrition, requiring not just tactical brilliance but an intimate understanding of the terrain. The SAS trained and worked with local Omani forces, providing intelligence, tracking, and tactical support. As they had in Malaya, the SAS adapted to the environment, using the mountains as a natural shield, moving in small teams, and striking with precision.

In Borneo, the SAS faced a different type of challenge. The island, rich in natural resources, was in the midst of a volatile period as Indonesia, under the leadership of Sukarno, attempted to incorporate the British territories of Sarawak and Sabah into the Indonesian republic. The conflict, known as the "Confrontation," pitted British and Commonwealth forces against Indonesian forces, many of whom were infiltrating Borneo's dense jungles and remote coastal areas.

Once again, the SAS's expertise in jungle warfare was invaluable. The SAS teams, working alongside Gurkhas and other special forces, executed covert raids against Indonesian positions. They worked in isolated, often hostile areas where the Indonesian forces could not rely on conventional military tactics. The SAS, always adaptable, responded with a combination of guerrilla tactics, sabotage, and psychological warfare. Their ability to strike swiftly and disappear into the dense foliage became their trademark.

Then came Aden, a conflict in the British colony of Yemen, which had become embroiled in a rebellion led by nationalist groups seeking independence. The SAS's involvement was vital in stabilising the region, as insurgents fought to expel the British and their colonial forces. Unlike the jungle warfare of Malaya and Borneo, the terrain here was characterised by the arid, urban environment of Aden itself, where the SAS adapted its tactics to focus more on urban counter-insurgency operations. They carried out ambushes, intelligence gathering, and sabotage missions, all while navigating the complexities of a city brimming with hostilities and divided loyalties.

These operations—the Dhofar Rebellion, the Indonesian Confrontation, and the Aden Emergency—were not isolated events but instead part of a broader shift in the role of special forces. The SAS, once a unit that had been designed for conventional warfare, was now firmly entrenched in the practice of counter-insurgency. Its soldiers were trained not just for combat but for the subtleties of politics, psychology, and diplomacy. They had come to understand that war was no longer simply a matter of battles and victories—it was a war for influence, for the hearts and minds of the people on the ground.

Strategies that Redefined Special Forces

The SAS's success in these campaigns would come to redefine the very concept of modern special forces. Unlike traditional military units, which relied on large-scale engagements and set-piece battles, the SAS operated in a way that was far more subtle, more strategic. They understood the terrain and the people; they knew that success was as much about perception and influence as it was about firepower.

One of the key innovations the SAS brought to modern warfare was the concept of "hearts and minds"—the understanding that local populations were as vital a resource as weapons or terrain. In each of the campaigns in Oman, Borneo, and Aden, the SAS worked closely with local forces, forging alliances, and sometimes even living within the communities they were protecting. They demonstrated that military victory could not be achieved by simply destroying an enemy—it was about winning the loyalty and trust of the people who had the power to turn the tide.

In these campaigns, the SAS also demonstrated a level of flexibility and innovation that was unmatched by any other force. The SAS soldier became the ultimate "warrior-diplomat" —trained to fight and to negotiate, to strike fear into the enemy and to win over the hearts of the oppressed. The boundaries between military, political, and social manoeuvring became increasingly blurred. This adaptability would later become the hallmark of special forces units across the world.

The legacy of these campaigns, the lessons learned in Borneo, Aden, and Oman, would go on to shape the future of modern special forces. But they also marked a pivotal moment in the history of the SAS itself—an organisation that had once been a band of misfits and outcasts, now firmly established as the elite unit of the British Army.

Chapter 5: Northern Ireland and The Troubles (1969–1998)

Covert Operations and Intelligence Gathering

The decade of the 1970s marked a turning point for the SAS. In its early years, the regiment had been defined by its daring desert raids, jungle warfare expertise, and strategic brilliance in far-flung territories. However, the 1960s and early 1970s brought a new, far more intimate type of conflict to the forefront of British military operations. This was a war fought not on distant battlefields, but on the very streets of the United Kingdom itself, in the shadow of history's most charged and divisive political conflict: The Troubles in Northern Ireland.

The Troubles, which began in earnest in 1969, were rooted in the long-standing political and sectarian divide between Catholics, who sought greater autonomy or independence for Northern Ireland, and Protestants, who remained loyal to the United Kingdom. What began as a series of civil rights protests quickly escalated into a violent conflict that saw the British Army deploy to Northern Ireland to keep the peace. The situation would quickly devolve, however, into a brutal and bloody insurgency against British rule.

In Northern Ireland, the SAS was thrust into a conflict of a different nature from anything it had previously encountered. The vast desert expanses and dense jungles were replaced by tight urban environments, where insurgents and civilians alike blurred the lines between friend and foe. The British Army, overwhelmed by the escalating violence, began to rely heavily on special forces—particularly the SAS—to engage the more elusive elements of the insurgency: the Provisional Irish Republican Army (IRA).

From the outset, the SAS was deployed in a clandestine role—focused on intelligence gathering, covert operations, and hunting down the IRA's key figures. The threat from the IRA was not one that could be confronted by conventional military units. The Irish nationalists used guerrilla tactics and terror, striking when least expected and melting back into the civilian population after every attack. In this urban setting, the SAS's tactics—adapted from its previous counter-insurgency experiences—proved invaluable.

The SAS's primary task was to infiltrate the IRA, uncover its cell structures, and neutralise its leadership. They worked closely with intelligence agencies, most notably MI5 and MI6, piecing together fragments of intelligence, listening to intercepted communications, and providing critical analysis of IRA operations. Their ability to blend into the landscape and operate covertly—whether in the urban streets of Belfast or the rural landscapes of Northern Ireland—allowed them to take the fight to the IRA in ways the traditional army could not.

Controversial Actions and Impact on British Policy

While the SAS's effectiveness in tackling the IRA is beyond question, their operations in Northern Ireland were not without controversy. In an environment where distinctions between combatants and non-combatants were often murky, accusations of brutality and heavy-handedness frequently followed the regiment's operations.

The most notorious and controversial incident came in 1987, with the SAS's involvement in the killing of IRA members in Gibraltar, an operation known as "Operation Flavius." The operation saw the SAS ambush and kill three IRA men who were plotting to bomb the British Army's headquarters in the region. While the operation was considered a success in terms of eliminating a key threat, it was widely criticised for the manner in which it was carried out. The IRA men were killed in what some believed to be an execution-style ambush, rather than a battle fought in the heat of combat. The incident would become a symbol of the murky ethical dilemmas that special forces face when operating in politically charged environments.

Despite these controversies, the SAS's role in Northern Ireland was pivotal. Their highly secretive and surgical operations ensured that key IRA figures were eliminated or captured, and their efforts were instrumental in securing intelligence that would thwart further attacks. The skill of the SAS in carrying out quick, precise raids, often at night, became legendary. The regiment honed its ability to strike decisively, neutralising targets with pinpoint accuracy, and withdrawing without leaving a trace.

It was the SAS's unparalleled proficiency in intelligence gathering, combined with their tactical brilliance, that allowed the British government to gain the upper hand over the IRA. Their operations—often invisible to the public but deadly to the enemy—sent a powerful message to the Provisional IRA: no matter how elusive or dangerous the enemy, the SAS would be there.

However, the controversy surrounding their actions in Northern Ireland led to lasting debates about the balance between security and civil liberties, particularly when it came to the conduct of covert operations. Many questioned whether the use of such extreme methods—especially in a region as politically volatile as Northern Ireland—was justified. But for the men of the SAS, the success of their mission was clear: they were there to ensure that the war against the IRA would not be lost. The work of the SAS, however, was not without its costs, and the consequences of their actions would have repercussions that lasted well beyond the Troubles themselves.

The Impact of the SAS on British Policy

The SAS's actions in Northern Ireland left an indelible mark on British military policy and counter-terrorism strategy. Their success in dealing with the IRA paved the way for their involvement in future high-risk operations. The British Army and government would come to increasingly rely on the SAS not only for covert operations in Northern Ireland, but also in other theatres of conflict across the globe.

Northern Ireland also marked a shift in the public's perception of the SAS. While their exploits had always been shrouded in secrecy, the regiment's growing role in counter-insurgency operations brought them into the public eye. Their actions, whether hailed as heroic or criticised as heavy-handed, became emblematic of the relentless, unyielding nature of modern warfare. The SAS had evolved from an elite group of soldiers serving in distant deserts and jungles to a symbol of Britain's determination to prevail in the most complex and morally ambiguous conflicts.

The legacy of the SAS in Northern Ireland would resonate in future generations of special forces soldiers, serving as both a model of operational excellence and a warning of the dangers of unchecked power. Yet, amid the controversies and complications, one thing remained certain: the SAS had proven itself as a force capable of meeting any challenge, no matter how brutal or complex.

Chapter 6: The Iranian Embassy Siege (1980)

A Nation Watches: The World's First Televised Counter-Terror Operation

By the dawn of the 1980s, the SAS had firmly established itself as Britain's preeminent special forces regiment, renowned for its unmatched expertise in counter-insurgency and covert warfare. Yet, for all its successes in the jungles of Malaya and the streets of Belfast, the regiment had never before faced an operation that would capture the world's attention in quite the way that the Iranian Embassy siege would.

On April 30, 1980, a group of six armed militants stormed the Iranian Embassy in London, taking 26 hostages and demanding the release of prisoners held in Iran. The siege quickly spiralled out of control, and the British government, under Prime Minister Margaret Thatcher, found itself facing an unprecedented crisis. The Iranian Embassy was in the heart of the British capital, its violent takeover sending shockwaves throughout the nation and the world.

The siege was not just a high-stakes hostage situation. It was a symbol of the volatile geopolitics of the time: Iran was in the midst of a revolution, and the Iranian government was on the defensive after the fall of the Shah. The British were caught in the crossfire, and what started as a simple hostage-taking quickly evolved into an international diplomatic and military crisis.

For the SAS, this was more than just another mission. It was the chance to prove their mettle on the world stage, to show the public and the international community the full extent of their training, precision, and resolve. For the hostages, it was a fight for survival, and for the SAS operatives poised to storm the embassy, it was a test of their ability to execute a delicate, high-stakes operation under the intense pressure of the world watching.

For six days, the world witnessed the drama unfold on television as the hostage-takers made increasingly impossible demands, and the British government struggled to resolve the situation through diplomatic means. But as the hours passed, it became clear that negotiations would not yield results. Time was running out, and the hostages' lives were hanging by a thread.

It was then that the decision was made. The SAS would go in.

Tactics, Triumph, and Public Acclaim

The operation, which would later be known as "Operation Nimrod," was a testament to the discipline, precision, and ruthlessness of the SAS. The storming of the embassy had to be executed with pinpoint accuracy. There could be no room for error: any misstep could lead to the deaths of the hostages or the failure of the entire mission. The SAS operatives knew they had one chance to get it right.

As the clock ticked down, SAS units positioned themselves around the embassy, each member meticulously planning their role in the attack. The soldiers knew that the world was watching, but more importantly, they knew that failure was not an option. The siege had already stretched on for days, and public patience was running thin. But it wasn't just public opinion at stake—it was national pride, and the reputation of Britain's elite forces.

At 3:30 pm on May 5, 1980, the SAS stormed the embassy. The operation was swift and decisive, an assault that had been meticulously planned down to the smallest detail. The team used a combination of flashbangs, explosives, and diversionary tactics to overwhelm the militants, neutralise their threats, and rescue the hostages. The speed and efficiency with which the SAS acted were staggering. Within minutes, five of the six terrorists had been killed, and the hostages were freed. One of the terrorists had been captured alive, a crucial source of intelligence for future operations.

The world watched in awe as the operation unfolded. For the first time, a counter-terrorist operation of such precision and scale was broadcast live on television, allowing millions of viewers to witness firsthand the power and professionalism of the SAS. The raid was a triumph not just for the regiment but for the entire British government. It was an unqualified success, executed with military brilliance and minimal collateral damage. The British public was filled with admiration for the SAS and their incredible professionalism, and the operation became an iconic moment in the history of modern counter-terrorism.

But behind the triumph lay a deeper truth: Operation Nimrod was not simply a showcase for the SAS's impressive skills. It was a reminder of the increasing threat of terrorism in the post-Cold War world, where the lines between political motivations, religious extremism, and pure violence had become ever more blurred. It was a world where governments would rely on specialised units like the SAS to act as the first and last line of defence against increasingly sophisticated and deadly terrorist organisations.

The operation's success came at a cost, however. While no hostages were killed, several were injured, and one SAS operative was wounded during the operation. But the mission was seen as an unparalleled success. It established the SAS as the gold standard in counter-terrorism operations, a standard that would influence not just the British military but special forces around the globe.

In the aftermath of the operation, the SAS's role in counter-terrorism became a focal point for discussion in military circles and beyond. It was clear that the regiment's abilities went far beyond traditional military warfare: they were experts in high-risk, high-stakes operations where timing, precision, and the ability to read and react to the ever-changing dynamics of a hostage situation were paramount. The Iranian Embassy siege proved that the SAS was not just a force of war—it was a force of crisis management.

In the years that followed, the legacy of Operation Nimrod would grow, becoming a symbol of everything the SAS represented: tactical brilliance, the protection of life, and the willingness to fight for freedom against the darkest forces in the world. The images of the SAS descending upon the embassy, the hostages safely freed, and the militants neutralised, would be forever etched in the public's memory as one of the greatest feats of modern counter-terrorism.

Chapter 7: The Falklands War (1982)

Preparing for the Assault on Pebble Island

In 1982, the British military faced a crisis far from home, one that would test the SAS in a new and entirely different environment. The Falklands War was a conflict sparked by Argentina's sudden invasion of the British Overseas Territories of the Falkland Islands, a remote archipelago in the South Atlantic. For the British government, the loss of the islands was unthinkable. For Argentina, it was an assertion of sovereignty over a group of islands they had long claimed as their own. And for the SAS, it was an opportunity to once again prove their mettle in a high-stakes military campaign.

The Falklands, located almost 8,000 miles from Britain, were far from a traditional battleground. But it was not the geography that presented the greatest challenge—it was the environment. The harsh winds, freezing temperatures, and rugged, unforgiving terrain of the islands would provide a stark contrast to the deserts and jungles the SAS had previously operated in. Yet, despite the challenges, the SAS was called upon to support British operations aimed at liberating the islands and repelling the Argentine invaders.

The SAS's first major task in the Falklands was to assist in intelligence gathering and sabotage missions. They were tasked with infiltrating the islands undetected and gathering vital information about Argentine positions, movements, and fortifications. Pebble Island, a strategically significant location in the Falklands, became the target of one of the regiment's most daring and effective operations.

The Argentine forces had established a well-defended airstrip on Pebble Island, a critical base for their attack aircraft, which posed a major threat to the British task force preparing to retake the islands. The SAS would have to infiltrate the island, destroy the aircraft on the ground, and retreat without leaving a trace of their presence. The operation required meticulous planning, perfect execution, and the courage to strike deep behind enemy lines.

In the days leading up to the mission, the SAS began to prepare for what would become a lightning-fast raid. They rehearsed their tactics on the rocky terrain of the British mainland, simulating the harsh conditions of the Falklands. The operation, known as *Operation Mikado*, would see the SAS travel across the sea under the cover of darkness, land on Pebble Island, and launch a surprise attack that would leave the Argentine forces reeling. It was a classic example of the SAS's ethos: a small, highly trained unit capable of taking on a much larger enemy force with speed, precision, and devastating impact.

The raid on Pebble Island was a striking success. Under cover of night, the SAS infiltrated the island, neutralising Argentine forces with lightning speed. Within hours, they had destroyed several aircraft on the ground, along with fuel and ammunition supplies, crippling Argentina's ability to launch air strikes. The British forces were able to secure a strategic advantage, while the Argentine forces were left in disarray. The operation was a masterclass in surprise and sabotage, carried out with the precision that had become synonymous with the SAS.

The SAS's Role in Intelligence and Sabotage

But the SAS's involvement in the Falklands War went far beyond just sabotage missions. As the conflict raged on, the regiment played a key role in intelligence-gathering operations. The SAS's expertise in reconnaissance, combined with their ability to operate in small, flexible teams, made them invaluable in the fog of war.

The regiment's operatives worked tirelessly to infiltrate enemy lines, gather intelligence, and provide crucial information to the British forces. Their work was often conducted behind enemy lines, where they would risk life and limb to capture vital data about the Argentine forces. The information they provided proved to be a key factor in British decision-making, allowing the British military to plan their next moves with greater precision and foresight.

One of the most important aspects of the SAS's role in the Falklands War was their ability to adapt to the environment. While much of the British military was focused on conventional warfare—on ships, tanks, and artillery—the SAS understood that the conflict in the Falklands was not going to be won by sheer firepower alone. The rugged terrain, the unpredictable weather, and the vast distances between military positions meant that success would rely heavily on intelligence, agility, and precision. And in this arena, the SAS excelled.

As the war progressed, the regiment was called upon to carry out a variety of missions, each requiring a unique set of skills. They conducted reconnaissance on Argentine naval and air units, raided enemy positions, and provided critical intelligence that helped to shape the British strategy. Their ability to operate covertly and without detection allowed them to gather information that was often crucial to the success of larger British operations.

The SAS also played a crucial role in providing support for the conventional military forces. In a war where every inch of ground was contested, the regiment's expertise in small-unit tactics and guerrilla warfare allowed them to harry the enemy, disrupt their supply lines, and create chaos behind their lines. The sheer unpredictability of the SAS's operations meant that the Argentine forces were never able to rest easy, knowing that at any moment, the SAS could strike.

Chapter 8: The Gulf War and Desert Operations

Scud-Hunting Behind Enemy Lines

The Gulf War of 1990-1991 was a conflict that fundamentally changed the landscape of modern warfare. It was a war fought with high-tech weaponry, precision strikes, and the overwhelming power of a coalition of forces led by the United States. For the SAS, the war represented a new kind of battlefield—one that would demand not only their expertise in conventional warfare but also their ability to operate in a vast, desert landscape under intense pressure.

The conflict began when Iraq, under the leadership of Saddam Hussein, invaded neighbouring Kuwait, sparking outrage from the international community. The United Nations condemned the invasion, and a coalition of nations—led by the United States—was formed to drive Iraqi forces out of Kuwait and restore the sovereignty of the small nation. The SAS, as part of the British contribution to the coalition forces, was tasked with a variety of high-risk operations behind enemy lines.

The desert terrain of Iraq and Kuwait posed a stark contrast to the jungles and mountains where the SAS had operated in the past. The vast, open spaces left little cover or concealment, and the intense heat made even basic operations a struggle. But the SAS was undeterred. Their training, which had always emphasised adaptability and resourcefulness, was tailor-made for this new kind of environment.

One of the most significant tasks the SAS was assigned was the hunt for Scud missiles. Iraq had developed and deployed Scud ballistic missiles, which were capable of carrying both conventional and chemical warheads, and their use represented a major threat to both coalition forces and civilian populations. The SAS was given the responsibility of locating and destroying these missile sites before they could be launched. This was no simple task. The Scud sites were hidden deep within the Iraqi desert, often in remote locations that were difficult to access and heavily guarded.

The SAS's response was swift and methodical. Operating in small, highly trained teams, they would infiltrate enemy territory, gather intelligence, and track the movements of Scud launchers. These operations often took place in the dead of night, as the SAS used their skills in desert navigation, stealth, and concealment to avoid detection by Iraqi forces. The stakes were high—if a Scud missile was launched, it could strike anywhere within the coalition's vast area of operations.

The SAS was instrumental in locating and neutralising Scud sites, often before the Iraqis even knew they had been targeted. The regiment's success in these operations was a testament to their training, discipline, and expertise in unconventional warfare. It also marked a new chapter in the SAS's history, as they operated at the cutting edge of modern military technology, using satellites, GPS systems, and advanced communication tools to conduct their missions.

Bravo Two Zero: A Story of Heroism and Survival

One of the most famous operations conducted by the SAS during the Gulf War was *Bravo Two Zero*, a mission that became one of the most iconic—and controversial—episodes in the regiment's history. The mission's objective was to infiltrate Iraq, gather intelligence, and destroy communication lines, all while evading detection by the enemy. The team, led by Sergeant Major Andy McNab, was dropped behind enemy lines in the early stages of the war, tasked with sabotaging Iraq's infrastructure and causing as much disruption as possible.

What followed was a harrowing tale of courage, survival, and endurance. The SAS team found themselves deep in enemy territory, their mission compromised by a series of unforeseen obstacles. As they moved through the desert, they were spotted by Iraqi forces, and what was meant to be a quick, stealthy operation turned into a fight for survival. Outnumbered, outgunned, and facing overwhelming odds, the team was forced to fight their way out of enemy territory.

Despite the hardships and setbacks, Bravo Two Zero's members showed extraordinary resilience. After days of evading capture, some of the team managed to escape and were rescued. However, the operation was costly, with several members of the team captured by Iraqi forces. The story of Bravo Two Zero became one of the most publicised SAS operations, and it raised questions about the challenges of modern warfare and the fine line between success and failure.

In the aftermath of the mission, the SAS faced intense scrutiny from both the public and the military establishment. While Bravo Two Zero had achieved its objective of gathering intelligence, the loss of life and the difficulties faced by the team cast a shadow over the operation. Nevertheless, the bravery and resourcefulness of the SAS team during Bravo Two Zero were undeniable. The mission reinforced the regiment's reputation as a force capable of achieving extraordinary feats in the face of seemingly insurmountable odds.

The SAS in the Gulf War: Adapting to Modern Warfare

The Gulf War marked a significant evolution in the role of the SAS, as the regiment adapted to the challenges of modern warfare. While the SAS had long been associated with guerrilla tactics, sabotage, and counter-insurgency operations, the Gulf War saw them working alongside conventional forces, employing a combination of cutting-edge technology and traditional special forces methods. The regiment's role in the conflict was crucial, with the SAS carrying out numerous operations that contributed to the success of the coalition forces.

Their work in the Gulf War demonstrated the versatility of the SAS, as they used their expertise in desert warfare to conduct reconnaissance, gather intelligence, and strike at key targets behind enemy lines. The Gulf War also showcased the regiment's ability to operate under extreme conditions, in an unfamiliar environment, and with limited resources. Whether hunting Scud missiles or infiltrating enemy strongholds, the SAS proved once again that they were among the most capable and adaptable special forces in the world.

The conflict also highlighted the importance of the SAS's ability to work in tandem with other military units. While the regiment was known for its independence and autonomy, the Gulf War saw them integrating seamlessly into larger operations, providing crucial intelligence and support to conventional forces. The success of the SAS in the Gulf War cemented their reputation as the ultimate force multiplier, capable of turning the tide of battle in the most challenging of circumstances.

Chapter 9: Post-9/11 Operations

Afghanistan: Hunting Al-Qaeda and the Taliban

The events of September 11, 2001, sent shockwaves across the globe. The world was irrevocably changed by the terrorist attacks on the United States, and the international community's response was swift and decisive. The United States, with the support of its allies, launched Operation Enduring Freedom, a military campaign aimed at dismantling the Al-Qaeda network and removing the Taliban from power in Afghanistan. For the SAS, this marked a new era of operations—one in which counter-terrorism and high-stakes missions against an elusive enemy in an unforgiving landscape would become their focus.

In the rugged mountains and vast deserts of Afghanistan, the SAS faced a new kind of warfare. The Taliban had ruled the country for years, creating a highly fortified network of strongholds in the remote regions of the country. Al-Qaeda, meanwhile, had entrenched itself in the mountain caves and valleys, making it incredibly difficult for conventional forces to root them out. The SAS, however, was well-suited to this kind of conflict. Their experience in unconventional warfare, desert operations, and counter-insurgency tactics gave them an edge as they embarked on what would become one of their most challenging campaigns.

The SAS's role in Afghanistan was multifaceted. They operated alongside the United States and other coalition forces, conducting a range of missions—from intelligence gathering and surveillance to direct action against high-value targets. The regiment's specialty in small-unit tactics allowed them to operate effectively in this harsh and unforgiving environment, often in teams of just a few men. These small teams would infiltrate Taliban-held territory, gather intelligence, and engage in precision strikes against enemy targets. Their work was often shrouded in secrecy, and the nature of the mission meant that they operated far from the eyes of the media and the public.

One of the SAS's most significant contributions in Afghanistan was their role in tracking down and neutralising high-profile members of Al-Qaeda. Operating in the remote and rugged mountains of the country, they used their expertise in reconnaissance and intelligence to locate key targets and provide critical information to the wider coalition forces. In a number of operations, the SAS was instrumental in capturing or killing high-ranking Taliban and Al-Qaeda operatives, significantly disrupting the enemy's ability to fight back.

Iraq: High-Value Targets and Urban Warfare

The SAS's role in Iraq was just as pivotal. Following the invasion of Iraq in 2003, the coalition forces quickly overthrew Saddam Hussein's regime, but what followed was a brutal insurgency that would test the limits of modern warfare. The situation in Iraq presented new challenges for the SAS, as they faced not only conventional enemy forces but also the rise of insurgent groups and sectarian violence.

The SAS's tactics in Iraq were refined to meet the needs of urban warfare and the fight against an irregular, highly mobile enemy. The regiment was tasked with tracking down high-value targets—members of Saddam Hussein's regime, as well as insurgent leaders who were orchestrating attacks against coalition forces and civilians. The SAS's ability to conduct covert operations in complex urban environments was crucial to the success of these missions. Whether operating in the streets of Baghdad or the surrounding countryside, the SAS used their knowledge of counter-insurgency tactics to disrupt the insurgent networks and weaken their grip on power.

One of the most notable operations of the Iraq war involving the SAS was the capture of Saddam Hussein's half-brother, Barzan

Ibrahim al-Tikriti, who had been one of the most senior members of the former regime. The SAS played a key role in gathering intelligence that led to his capture, which was a significant blow to the insurgency and a major victory for coalition forces. The ability to target high-value individuals was one of the key strategies the SAS employed in Iraq, and their success in this area made a substantial impact on the overall military strategy in the region.

But urban warfare in Iraq was fraught with difficulties. The dense, chaotic environment made it easy for insurgents to blend in with the civilian population, and the SAS had to balance the need for swift action with the requirement to minimise collateral damage. This was a delicate and often dangerous task, requiring precise intelligence, careful planning, and flawless execution.

The SAS's role in Iraq was not without its controversy, however. As with previous conflicts, the regiment's covert operations sometimes crossed ethical lines, and their actions were often the subject of intense scrutiny. While their missions were successful in targeting insurgents and high-value individuals, the use of extreme measures in some operations raised questions about the limits of special forces operations and the blurred lines between legal and illegal warfare.

Afghanistan and Iraq: The Changing Face of Warfare

The post-9/11 conflicts in Afghanistan and Iraq marked a significant shift in the nature of modern warfare. No longer were the SAS engaged in conventional military operations against regular armies. Instead, they faced a complex web of insurgents, terrorists, and non-state actors. The landscape was constantly shifting, and the rules of engagement were constantly evolving.

For the SAS, this meant adapting to a new kind of warfare—one that demanded a combination of high-tech intelligence, rapid response, and an intimate knowledge of the cultural and political landscape. The regiment's ability to operate with autonomy, often in secret, meant that they were able to execute highly sensitive missions without the same level of oversight as conventional forces.

In both Afghanistan and Iraq, the SAS's effectiveness was driven by their deep knowledge of the terrain, their ability to work in small, highly mobile teams, and their mastery of unconventional warfare tactics. These qualities enabled them to operate in environments where other forces might have struggled, and they allowed the SAS to maintain their reputation as one of the most effective special forces units in the world.

As the wars in Afghanistan and Iraq dragged on, the SAS's role continued to evolve. They became increasingly involved in counter-terrorism operations, working closely with intelligence agencies to track down Al-Qaeda and other extremist groups. Their missions were often highly classified, and their successes were rarely publicised. But their work was essential to the broader coalition effort, and their ability to strike at the heart of the enemy made a real difference on the ground.

The Enduring Legacy of SAS Operations

The post-9/11 operations in Afghanistan and Iraq reinforced the enduring legacy of the SAS. Their ability to adapt to new threats, employ cutting-edge technology, and operate with precision and stealth made them indispensable in the modern battlefield. Whether hunting down Al-Qaeda operatives in the mountains of Afghanistan or conducting covert operations in the cities of Iraq, the SAS remained a force to be reckoned with.

As the world continues to grapple with the challenges of modern warfare, the lessons learned by the SAS in these conflicts will undoubtedly continue to shape the future of special forces operations. Their commitment to excellence, adaptability, and unwavering dedication to their missions ensures that the SAS remains a vital force in the fight against terrorism and global instability.

Chapter 10: Training, Selection, and the Making of an SAS Soldier

The Brutal Selection Process

Becoming a member of the SAS is not for the faint of heart. It is a journey that demands not only extraordinary physical endurance but also mental resilience, exceptional intelligence, and the ability to thrive under the most extreme conditions. The process of selection is infamous for its brutality, and only the strongest, most capable candidates make it through. For every man who earns the right to wear the coveted beret, countless others are left behind in the unforgiving landscape of the British countryside, broken by the pressure, the pain, and the relentless demands placed upon them.

Selection for the SAS is a rigorous process designed to test every aspect of a potential recruit's character and ability. It begins with the infamous "Endurance Course," a 40-mile march across mountainous terrain, carrying a full pack, in a set time frame. The march is followed by a series of tests designed to challenge the mind as much as the body—night navigation exercises, endurance tests, and stress-inducing operations designed to simulate the pressure of combat.

But it is not just physical prowess that the SAS requires. Mental fortitude is key. Throughout the selection process, candidates are subjected to psychological stress designed to break them down and then build them back up. They must demonstrate the ability to think clearly and make decisions under extreme pressure. A mistake in decision-making could cost lives, and the SAS requires that its soldiers remain calm, focused, and rational at all times, no matter the circumstances.

Perhaps the most gruelling aspect of the selection process is the "hills phase," which is a series of long, arduous marches designed to break down the body's defenses and test a candidate's limits. The marches take place over several days, and candidates are given minimal rest or food. The unforgiving hills and constant physical exertion push men to their breaking point. The men who make it through are those who can overcome not only the physical pain but also the mental strain. They are the ones who refuse to quit, even when every muscle in their body screams for relief.

Jungle, Mountain, and Arctic Warfare Training

Once a candidate has passed the selection process, they begin a series of specialised training courses that prepare them for the diverse and challenging environments they will encounter during operational deployments. This phase of training is designed to ensure that an SAS soldier is prepared for combat in any terrain, from dense jungles to frozen mountain ranges.

Jungle warfare training is particularly demanding. The humid, oppressive heat of the jungle can wear down even the most seasoned soldiers, and the dense foliage presents constant challenges. The SAS trains in some of the most hostile jungles in the world, from the rainforests of Malaysia to the jungles of South America. Soldiers are taught how to navigate without the use of conventional maps, relying instead on natural landmarks and the stars. They learn how to build shelters, forage for food, and survive in an environment that is both alien and lethal. Perhaps the most important lesson learned in the jungle is patience. The jungle can be both merciless and unforgiving, but the SAS knows that stealth, discipline, and the ability to blend into the environment are the keys to survival and success.

Mountain warfare training is equally intense. Soldiers are taught to operate in extreme cold, high altitudes, and the harshest of weather conditions. They must learn to traverse treacherous mountain ranges while carrying heavy equipment and supplies, all while battling the effects of altitude sickness and extreme fatigue. The SAS's ability to operate in the mountains is essential, as many of the world's most volatile regions, from the mountains of Afghanistan to the peaks of the Andes, are home to insurgents and terrorists. The skills learned in mountain warfare training are often the difference between life and death.

Arctic warfare training is the final phase, where soldiers are taught to endure and survive in the frozen wilderness. In this environment, the SAS must learn how to navigate through thick snow, survive in sub-zero temperatures, and adapt to the harshest of elements. Every aspect of their training is designed to prepare them for the extremes of survival—skills that are essential when fighting in cold and inhospitable regions. The mental fortitude required to endure these conditions is immense, and it is a testament to the soldiers' resilience that they emerge from this training ready for anything.

Resistance to Interrogation

The SAS places a strong emphasis on psychological resilience and resistance to interrogation. In many special forces operations, soldiers are captured or placed in situations where they may be interrogated by the enemy. The ability to withstand physical and mental torture is crucial, not only for the safety of the soldier but also for the success of the mission. The SAS trains its operatives to resist interrogation using a combination of techniques designed to maintain mental clarity and discipline.

The training includes psychological preparation, where soldiers are taught how to control their thoughts and emotions, avoid giving away sensitive information, and maintain a sense of calm under duress. It also includes practical exercises in which soldiers are subjected to simulated interrogation techniques. These exercises are designed to push soldiers to the brink, forcing them to confront their deepest fears and the possibility of their own capture.

The focus is on developing a mindset that refuses to yield to pressure, no matter the circumstances. SAS soldiers are trained to endure, to resist, and to survive in the face of unimaginable stress. They are taught that the success of their mission—and the safety of their comrades—depends on their ability to maintain control and withhold critical information, no matter what.

The Making of an SAS Soldier

Becoming an SAS soldier is a transformative experience. The selection and training process shapes not only the body but the mind, forging individuals who are capable of enduring the most extreme conditions and performing feats that most people could not even imagine. It is a process of personal growth, where candidates are pushed to their limits and beyond, forced to confront their weaknesses and develop strengths they never knew they had.

An SAS soldier is not just a trained warrior; he is a master of his own mind. The mental toughness and resilience that are cultivated through the selection process and training allow SAS soldiers to operate in the most challenging and dangerous environments on the planet. They are individuals who have not only survived physical hardships but have developed the psychological strength to succeed under the most intense pressure.

Through this brutal yet transformative process, the SAS produces soldiers who are capable of extraordinary feats—men who can operate behind enemy lines, carry out covert missions, and face danger with unshakable resolve. They are the epitome of elite special forces, and their training, selection, and the making of them are what sets them apart as the best of the best.

Chapter 11: The SAS in Popular Culture

Films, Books, and Games Inspired by the SAS

The Special Air Service (SAS), with its rich and storied history of daring operations and covert missions, has become an icon in the world of popular culture. The SAS's aura of invincibility and its association with the highest levels of military expertise have made it a constant source of inspiration for filmmakers, writers, and video game developers. Whether it is on the silver screen, in the pages of best-selling novels, or in the virtual world of gaming, the SAS is a symbol of bravery, skill, and unparalleled toughness.

One of the earliest representations of the SAS in popular culture came through the pen of former SAS soldier, **Chris Ryan**. His autobiographical accounts and novels, particularly *The One That Got Away*—which recounted his harrowing escape from an Iraqi ambush during the Gulf War—brought the SAS's true-to-life heroism into the public eye. Ryan's experience was emblematic of the SAS's ethos, which holds that each member is a master of self-reliance and perseverance, capable of surviving against all odds.

In the world of cinema, the SAS's exploits have been dramatised in numerous films. Perhaps the most iconic of these is **"Who Dares Wins" (1982)**, a British action film that blends real-life SAS tactics with fictional adventure. The film follows an SAS team on a mission to rescue hostages held by a radical group, and while it may be fictional, it successfully captures the spirit of the unit's approach to combat—stealth, precision, and lethal efficiency. This film, in particular, helped to cement the association of the SAS with the phrase "Who Dares Wins," a slogan that remains synonymous with the regiment to this day.

Other films such as **"The Delta Force" (1986)** and **"Six Days Seven Nights" (1998)** also featured SAS characters, often as part of an elite team undertaking high-risk rescue missions. These films perpetuated the image of the SAS as a force of unparalleled toughness, capable of taking on even the most dangerous missions in hostile environments.

Television, too, has embraced the mystique of the SAS. The popular British reality series **"SAS: Who Dares Wins"** brought the regiment's selection process to the public's attention in a new and engaging way. Contestants—often from civilian backgrounds—are subjected to a series of gruelling tasks and challenges designed to test their physical and mental limits, simulating the real-life selection process that SAS candidates endure. While the show is entertainment, it offers a glimpse into the intense training and discipline that the SAS recruits undergo, offering viewers a deeper understanding of the qualities required to join one of the world's most elite military forces.

Books, too, have played an essential role in the public's understanding of the SAS. Beyond Chris Ryan's work, **Andy McNab**, another former SAS operative, published his semi-autobiographical *Bravo Two Zero* in 1993, recounting his time behind enemy lines in Iraq during the Gulf War. The book details the failed mission, the harrowing escape, and McNab's resilience in the face of unimaginable odds. McNab's subsequent fiction series, most notably the *Nick Stone* novels, further embedded the image of the SAS as a unit capable of extraordinary feats of daring and survival. In these books, SAS soldiers are portrayed as not only skilled warriors but also highly trained individuals who can think their way out of the most complex situations. The books quickly became bestsellers, further propelling the SAS's image as the epitome of elite military force.

The influence of the SAS extends beyond literature and film. In the realm of video games, the SAS has been portrayed as the ideal representation of special forces excellence. One of the most popular franchises to feature the SAS is **"Call of Duty"**, where players can take control of SAS operatives in numerous missions around the world. The series, known for its realistic combat scenarios and tactical gameplay, frequently draws upon the SAS's real-world reputation to craft thrilling and immersive experiences. The appearance of SAS characters in games such as **"Rainbow Six Siege"** and **"Counter-Strike"** has further solidified the group's cultural presence, with players around the world seeking to emulate the stealth, precision, and teamwork that the SAS is known for.

While these representations are often dramatised or fictionalised for entertainment purposes, they capture the essence of the SAS's global reputation. The regiment's willingness to tackle any mission, regardless of the odds, is a trait that resonates deeply with the public. However, the portrayal of the SAS is not always completely accurate. While these depictions highlight the regiment's bravery and professionalism, they sometimes fail to show the personal toll such intense work can take on the soldiers. The real SAS soldier is not merely a perfect warrior but a man who deals with the psychological aftermath of combat, with the burden of guilt, trauma, and loss often weighing heavily on their minds.

The Myth and the Reality

The SAS's mystique is a double-edged sword. On one hand, it has made the regiment one of the most respected special forces units in the world, with its soldiers hailed as the best of the best. On the other hand, it has led to a proliferation of myths and misconceptions about the unit. The line between fact and fiction can often blur, and this is partly the result of the regiment's high level of secrecy, which has only fuelled speculation.

The SAS's official motto, "Who Dares Wins," is itself a rallying cry for the brave and the bold, yet it can also be misinterpreted as a symbol of reckless abandon. In reality, the SAS embodies the highest levels of precision, discipline, and professionalism, qualities that ensure success in even the most challenging operations. While the idea of a lone hero charging headlong into danger may be appealing in films and books, the true success of the SAS lies in its collaborative approach to mission planning, its meticulous attention to detail, and its ability to think several steps ahead of the enemy.

The real SAS soldier is not a fictional hero but an individual who has undergone years of gruelling training, who operates as part of a well-oiled team, and who is capable of extraordinary feats of courage. The reality of the SAS may not always match the mythology, but it is every bit as impressive.

The legacy of the SAS—shaped by decades of service, sacrifice, and success—continues to influence both the world of elite special forces and popular culture. From books and films to video games and documentaries, the SAS's stories continue to captivate audiences, shaping the public's understanding of what it means to be a member of the world's most elite fighting force.

Chapter 12: Legacy and Influence

Global Special Forces Modelled on the SAS

The enduring legacy of the Special Air Service (SAS) extends far beyond the United Kingdom. As the world's preeminent special forces unit, the SAS has inspired the creation and evolution of similar elite forces in countries across the globe. From the United States to Australia, from Canada to Israel, military institutions have looked to the SAS as a model of excellence in counter-terrorism, hostage rescue, reconnaissance, and direct action missions.

Perhaps the most well-known of these is the **United States Army's Delta Force**, officially known as the 1st Special Forces Operational Detachment-Delta (SFOD-D). Created in 1977, Delta Force was directly influenced by the SAS's tactical innovation and operational success. The selection process, which is infamous for its gruelling physical and mental demands, mirrors the SAS's approach to evaluating potential candidates. Likewise, Delta Force operators undergo extensive training in unconventional warfare, hostage rescue, and counter-terrorism—skills that the SAS perfected in the heat of battle.

Another unit inspired by the SAS is the **Australian Special Air Service Regiment (SASR)**, which was formed in 1957 with direct assistance from the British SAS. The Australian SASR modelled its operations, training, and ethos on the British regiment, adopting many of the same methods for unconventional warfare and counter-insurgency. Over the decades, the Australian SAS has proven itself in numerous conflicts, including Vietnam, Iraq, and Afghanistan, often working alongside British and American forces. The regiment's relationship with the SAS remains close, with regular exchanges of knowledge and training between the two forces.

Israel's **Sayeret Matkal**, the elite special forces unit of the Israeli Defence Forces (IDF), also traces its roots to the SAS. Formed in 1957, Sayeret Matkal was heavily influenced by British methods of warfare, particularly in the realm of deep reconnaissance and counter-terrorism. The unit's most famous operation, the rescue of hostages from a hijacked airliner in Entebbe, Uganda, in 1976, demonstrated the same calculated precision and operational excellence that the SAS had long been known for. Like the SAS, Sayeret Matkal operates with a high degree of autonomy, relying on rapid deployment, stealth, and the ability to execute complex missions in hostile environments.

Other countries with special forces units inspired by the SAS include **Canada's Joint Task Force 2 (JTF2)**, **France's GIGN (National Gendarmerie Intervention Group)**, and **Germany's Kommando Spezialkräfte (KSK)**. Each of these units, while unique in its own right, has taken cues from the SAS in terms of training, mission specialisation, and the rigorous mental and physical endurance required to succeed in such demanding roles.

The influence of the SAS on global special forces is undeniable. The regiment's training methods, operational philosophies, and ethos have set a benchmark for excellence. Its tactics, honed over decades of real-world combat, have been adopted and adapted by numerous forces, ensuring that the SAS's legacy lives on in military units around the world.

The Enduring Power of Who Dares Wins

The phrase "Who Dares Wins" is synonymous with the SAS. It encapsulates the essence of the regiment: a fearless, unyielding spirit that drives its soldiers to tackle the most dangerous and seemingly impossible missions. The motto, adopted in 1941 by the unit's founder, David Stirling, has become more than just a rallying cry—it is a philosophy that defines the SAS and its members.

This philosophy of daring to take on challenges that others deem impossible has resonated far beyond the battlefield. It has permeated popular culture, inspiring countless individuals across all walks of life. The SAS's approach to problem-solving, characterised by adaptability, precision, and boldness, has found echoes in the business world, in sports, and in everyday life. The ethos of "Who Dares Wins" is about taking calculated risks, trusting in one's training and instincts, and pushing through adversity—traits that have universal appeal.

But the enduring power of "Who Dares Wins" lies not just in its inspirational quality but in its connection to a deep and profound truth: it is the product of decades of real-world experience, borne out of necessity. The SAS was born out of the brutal and unforgiving desert campaigns of World War II, where the margin for error was razor-thin and the cost of failure was often death. The success of the SAS's operations—whether in the sands of North Africa or the jungles of Malaya—was built on the willingness of its men to take bold, calculated risks when others would hesitate. In this way, the motto is more than a slogan—it is a reflection of the real, often dangerous, work of the regiment.

Today, the SAS stands as a symbol of military excellence and personal bravery. Its legacy is not only one of tactical innovation and operational success but also of the extraordinary men who have served within its ranks. These soldiers, many of whom remain anonymous, embody the values that have come to define the regiment: courage, discipline, and an unflinching commitment to the mission. Their stories—often untold, but never forgotten—are a testament to the indomitable spirit that drives the SAS.

In the modern world, the SAS continues to adapt to new threats, from the rise of global terrorism to the challenges of cyber warfare. Yet, the core principles that have guided the regiment for over 80 years remain unchanged. The SAS's legacy is not just in its past successes, but in its ongoing commitment to staying at the forefront of military innovation, to never resting on its laurels, and to always being ready for whatever challenges lie ahead.

As long as there are those who dare to face the impossible, the spirit of the SAS will endure. "Who Dares Wins" is not merely a motto; it is a legacy that will continue to inspire generations to come.

Conclusion

Reflections on the Unwavering Spirit of the SAS

The story of the SAS is one woven with threads of extraordinary bravery, innovation, and an unyielding will to overcome the impossible. From its daring inception in the deserts of North Africa to its ongoing operations across the globe, the regiment has defined what it means to confront adversity head-on. Its soldiers, marked by an almost otherworldly blend of resilience, resourcefulness, and tactical brilliance, have shaped not only the course of military history but also the very fabric of modern special forces.

At its core, the SAS embodies the very essence of warfare itself: a constant evolution driven by necessity. Over the decades, the regiment has adapted, innovated, and perfected its methods, never resting on its laurels, always pushing the boundaries of what is possible. In each mission—whether fighting behind enemy lines, conducting covert operations, or rescuing hostages from the jaws of terror—the SAS has displayed a unique combination of daring risk-taking and meticulous precision.

But the legacy of the SAS is not merely written in the annals of military campaigns. It extends far beyond the confines of battlefields and war zones, having shaped the world in ways that resonate with those who seek to lead, to innovate, or to overcome their own personal obstacles. The regiment's values —discipline, bravery, and above all, the indomitable will to succeed against all odds—serve as a beacon of inspiration for individuals everywhere, from military personnel to ordinary citizens striving to push past their limits.

The motto "Who Dares Wins" is not just a catchphrase; it is the crystallisation of the SAS's spirit. It reflects a profound truth: that courage is not the absence of fear, but the willingness to face it.

The SAS does not seek to avoid danger, but to master it—transforming fear into focus and uncertainty into action. This relentless pursuit of excellence, this refusal to back down in the face of adversity, continues to inspire not just soldiers, but anyone willing to rise to the occasion and meet life's challenges with resolve.

As we reflect on the remarkable history of the SAS, we are reminded of the cost of its success: the countless sacrifices made by those who served in its ranks, many of whom remain unsung heroes. Yet, their stories are immortalised in the ethos of the regiment, a testament to the extraordinary character of the men and women who have donned the coveted wings of the SAS. Their courage and determination have not only shaped the history of warfare but have left an indelible mark on the world.

In the end, the spirit of the SAS is not bound by time, nor by borders. It is a force that transcends the battlefield, a legacy of courage and resilience that will continue to inspire future generations to dare greatly, to confront the impossible, and to never give up in the face of overwhelming odds.

The SAS may have begun as a small, unconventional force, born of desperation in the darkest days of war—but its impact on history, and on the very idea of what it means to be truly elite, will echo for as long as the stories of bravery and triumph continue to be told.

"Who Dares Wins" is not simply the motto of the SAS; it is the very heart of its legacy.